AMERICANS ON THE MOVE

Elizabeth Laird

A HISTORY OF TRAVEL

The history of the United States is a story of people on the move. The Native Americans came to North America many thousands of years ago. Some of them built villages and stayed there, but many moved from place to place. They followed the buffalo and lived in tents.

The first travelers from Europe came to live in an unknown land. At first, they stayed near the coast, but then a few brave men went west, far into the country. Two of them were Meriwether Lewis and William Clark. In 1804, they started on their long journey from St. Louis, Missouri, to the Pacific Ocean. They followed the Missouri River west, went across the Rocky Mountains, and followed the Columbia River to the Pacific. Then, they turned around, and traveled back to St. Louis. It was a great journey.

During the next 150 years, millions of poor people came from the old cities of Europe. They built the new cities of the U.S., and farmed the land. But they did not always stay in their new cities or on their farms. Many people moved on, deeper and deeper into the new land.

Some followed religious leaders like Joseph Smith. He and his followers, the Mormons, built Salt Lake City in Utah. Others went to look for gold. After the California Gold Rush, in 1849, San Francisco grew from a village to a city in only a few years.

Even in the 1930s, large numbers of people were still on the move. In Oklahoma, the first farmers found good land. They grew wheat, wheat, and more wheat. But after a few years, the land was tired. Nothing grew anymore. Oklahoma farmers, the "Okies," had to move on.

Many went to California. They looked for work on the big new fruit farms in the California Valley.

Perhaps you think that this is all history. Not at all. People are still moving to the U.S. and finding new homes there. Up to one million people come into the United States from Mexico in one year. At the same time, many more arrive from the Pacific nations, from the Philippines, Korea, Vietnam, Taiwan, and also from Central and South America.

The history of the U.S. is still on the move.

Far left: Nineteenth-century pioneers going west through the Rocky Mountains.

Left: Italians arriving at Ellis Island, New York, in the 1880s.

Above: Oklahoma farmers lost everything in the 1930s. Many moved on to California.

HIGHWAYS ACROSS AMERICA

There is a moving van outside the Jacksons' house today. The Jacksons are moving—again. Mr. Jackson has a new job, in another state. He's going to make more money. He and his wife have bought a bigger house. The children will go to new schools, and Mrs. Jackson will look for a new job too.

The Jacksons are like most of their friends. They often move to a new house, a new town, or a new state. Half of all American families move into a different house every five years.

It's a long way to the Jacksons' new home. The moving van will go on one of the U.S.'s great interstate

highways. Four of these roads cross North America from east to west. The Jacksons will travel along I (Interstate) 80. It goes from the George Washington Bridge in New Jersey to San Francisco, California.

The Jacksons will drive to their new home by car. The trip will take two or three days. You cannot drive more than 65 miles per hour on American roads. And the roads are so long that drivers often get sleepy.

At night, the Jacksons will stop at a motel. It will be quite cheap, and clean. Perhaps it will be a Holiday Inn. There is a Holiday Inn in almost every town and city in the U.S. They are all the same. They all have the same kind of menu in the restaurant and the same furniture in the rooms.

"The best surprise is no surprise," says Holiday Inn. They like you to find what you expect.

On all American roads, you can expect the same signs too. The green ones show the names of places. The blue ones show gas stations, restaurants, and motels.

Interstate 80 is a very long highway, but it is never empty. The Jacksons will meet thousands of other automobiles. Inside some, there will be other families on the move. Some will be old people, who want to live in sunny California.

Others will be young people who want to study in another city. There will be parents who want to live near their grown-up children. And there will be people moving to new jobs— people like the Jacksons.

Left: A highway in Arizona.
Above: Signs on Interstate 80.

AUTOMOBILES

Why do Americans love automobiles more than most other things? Is it because they need them? Maybe. In many places in the U.S., people can travel only by car. Maybe it's because of the cars' wonderful names—Cadillac, Pontiac, Buick, Chevrolet. Or maybe it's because many American cars are so big and beautiful. Americans are buying more small cars now, but their cars are often much bigger than foreign ones.

There are 160 million automobiles on American roads. Some people feel that there are too many. They are tired of waiting in traffic jams. They can never find a place to park.

It's too late now. You can't take the cars away. Most modern cities

have many big roads, but few trains or buses. Modern houses are often a long way from schools and stores. Cars are necessary to many people now.

Detroit is the center of the American automobile industry. The factory managers of Detroit understand that most Americans want to buy new cars often. Many families sell their old car once a year and buy another. They want the newest and the best.

Automobiles can tell you a lot about people. Whose is that fast little sportscar? It belongs to a young businesswoman. She works in the center of a large city. She needs to drive quickly and park easily. Whose is that big, old-fashioned pick-up truck with the broken door? It belongs to a farmer who lives miles away from town. He needs to carry machines, animals, and all kinds of things in the back of his pick-up. And what's that long pink car with the red pool on the back? It's a "stretch limo" for a very rich person with funny ideas.

The most important person travels not with one but with many cars. The U.S. President goes in a "motorcade." There are motorcycles in the front with blue lights and loud sirens. After them come the President's bodyguards. The President's automobile has glass doors and windows strong enough to stop bullets.

I was right, wasn't I? Automobiles can tell you a lot about people.

Top left: A Cadillac in New York.

Bottom left: A farmer's family with their pick-up truck.

Above: A stretch limo with a pool on the back.

THE GREAT AMERICAN TRAFFIC JAM

What is worse than no cars at all? Too many cars, of course. That's the problem in many American cities. In Los Angeles, it's awful. There's just too much traffic. When there are big traffic jams, miles and miles of cars stop moving, and the air becomes thick and dirty. It hurts your eyes and makes you cough.

Californians are always talking about traffic. It's not surprising. Some people take four hours to drive to work and four hours to drive home again. Sometimes there are still traffic jams at 2 o'clock in the morning.

But Los Angeles is in California, and Californians like to find answers to all their problems. Their cars, they say, are a kind of home. Alone in your car, it is quiet and you have time to think. When you are sitting in a traffic jam, there are many things you can do. Some people brush their teeth and shave. Other people have breakfast or a long, slow lunch. You can also learn a language, or play your trumpet, or

sunbathe, or call your office on your car phone.

Business must go on, even when there are traffic jams. Some big companies in cities like New York and Washington use bicycle messengers. Bicycles can go quickly in and out of lines of traffic. They can carry important letters and papers faster than cars can.

Bicycle messengers are young, usually under eighteen years old. They ride fast between cars and taxis. Some of them wear feathers in their helmets, and very colorful shirts and shoes. They are paid well because their job is very dangerous. Sadly, some get hurt in accidents.

America's traffic problems won't go away. Even schools often do not have enough parking places because a lot of teenagers drive their cars to school.

American schools have many other problems. People say that too many children never learn to read and write. Some know little or nothing about history or geography. But almost all children learn an important American lesson. They learn how to drive a car.

Far left: Traffic in Los Angeles.
Left: A bicycle messenger in Washington, D.C.
Above: A school parking lot.

MOBILE HOMES

The great historic places of the Old World are cities, castles, and gardens. But in the New World, some of the most interesting historic places are the roads. Americans remember the great journeys of their history in movies, stories, and pictures. Their great-grandparents crossed America on horses and in wagons. They went along lonely and dangerous roads, or "trails": the Santa Fe Trail, the Oregon Trail, the Old Chisholm Trail.

"Go west, young man," fathers said to their sons. And they did.

They still do—on vacation. They don't go in wagons now, of course. They go in mobile homes. Some mobile homes are pulled by the family car. Some, like Winnebagos, have a driver's cab. Behind the cab is a room with beds, a small kitchen, a table, and a washing place. Winnebagos are great for vacations. A family can travel in the Winnebago, and stop at campgrounds to sleep and eat. They do not have to spend money on motels. In summer, the campgrounds in the national parks are full of mobile homes.

American factories make new and better mobile homes all the time. Some of them are palaces on wheels. But the idea is not a new one. In the 1930s, there were a large number of "Airstreamers" on the road. These wonderful old mobile homes looked like small space ships. They were made of shiny silver

metal. Sometimes you can still see them out on the highways.

Mobile homes are not only for vacations. Many people live in them. Five percent of all American homes started as mobile homes. But many of them do not travel anymore. They are parked in trailer parks. People build on new rooms, and grow flowers and trees near them. Soon the mobile homes look like houses. The difference is that mobile homes are much cheaper than houses. Most Americans can buy one.

Americans like to move. They like to feel that they can leave town and go on, to a new place and a new life. They like to feel free. A mobile home feels like a ticket to freedom, even one that never leaves its trailer park.

Left: Mobile homes go everywhere, north, south, east, and west. This one is in the far north, in Alaska.

Above: Airstreamer owners like to meet sometimes. Here they are at Louisville, Kentucky.

LOW RIDERS

Some people like cars. Some people love them. Some people can't live without them. There are a lot of people like that, down in New Mexico. They are called "low riders" because their cars can "ride" very "low." When they go around corners, the bottom of the car touches the road. That's not always a good idea, so low riders have special machines in the cars to lift them higher off the ground.

The low riders of New Mexico spend all their free time working on their cars. When the car is perfect, it can go to rallies and win prizes. But first, there's a lot to do.

Most low riders buy old cars— from the 1940s, 50s, and 60s. Then they paint the outside in wonderful colors. Sometimes they paint beautiful patterns and pictures inside the car too. They cover the inside with soft material, like fur and velvet. Then the real fun begins.

A low rider thinks and dreams about his car all the time. Then he makes his dream come true.

At a low-rider rally, most people speak Spanish or "Spanglish," half

Spanish, half English. They spend a lot of time looking at all the cars. Then they choose the best one. It's a great day for the winner. He will probably get a silver cup.

When the rally is finished, the low riders will drive away. But they won't go home yet. First they will drive up and down the main street of town. When you've done all that work, you want other people to see and enjoy it too.

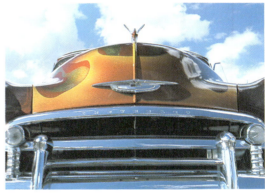

Far left: Inside a low-rider car.
Left: Cars and drivers at a low-rider rally in New Mexico.
Above: Details from the outside of a car.

PETERBILTS AND CB RADIO

Some people think that works of art are only in museums and art galleries. They're wrong. There are works of art driving across America all the time. From far away, they don't look like works of art. They only look like trucks. But if you go near, you will see that they are beautiful. They have bright colors and shiny metal, and some have wonderful pictures on them too.

There are bad trucks and good trucks, but the kings of them all are the Peterbilts. These are wonderful machines—strong, good-looking, and comfortable inside. They need to be. The U.S. is a very, very big country. Truckers often spend weeks on the road. They carry fruit from California and wheat from Kansas. They take steel to Detroit and gasoline to Los Angeles. Their drivers sometimes stay away from home for months. They often sleep in the cab of their truck. Modern trucks have a little room in the cab, behind the driver's seat. In it there is a bed and a place for clothes. Some trucks have TVs and refrigerators.

It is often lonely on the road. Most truckers have a radio in their cab. They can listen to and talk to other drivers. This kind of radio is called "Citizens' Band." People use

it for all kinds of things. Lonely people make friends. Drivers tell others about dangers on the road. Lovers talk together. Some people use their CB radio to plan crimes. Others use it to help the police catch criminals. It's all there—all of life is there on CB radio.

American truck drivers go through all kinds of weather. There's the deep snow of winter in the North. There's the burning sun of the great deserts in the Southwest. There are high winds in Michigan and tornados in Florida. But you don't see many dirty trucks on American roads. Most drivers wash them once a day. The colors stay beautiful, and the metal shines in the sun.

Left: A Peterbilt truck, bright and clean and ready to go.
Top right: A truck driver talking on CB radio.
Bottom right: The truck driver's bed in the cab behind the driving seat.

GETTING AROUND THE BIG APPLE

They call New York "the Big Apple." Maybe it's not exactly like an apple, but it's certainly very big. There are too many people, that's the problem. The streets are always full of cars and trucks, and you can never find a place to park.

If you have enough money, you can take a taxi. New York cabs are yellow. They all look the same. But the drivers are very different. Some were born and raised in New York, but many are newcomers to the United States. There are Indian, Pakistani, Sicilian, Vietnamese, African, and Mexican drivers. A few drive slowly, but most go very, very fast.

Cab driving is a difficult job. It can be dangerous too. Thieves often try to steal the drivers' money. Drivers sometimes get hurt. One cab driver, John Feyko, got tired of it. He wanted to do something different. So he became an animal cab driver. He takes pet cats, dogs, birds, and even snakes to the park or to the animal hospital. There are a lot of rich people in New York. They want the best, even for their animals. They are happy to pay for a special animal cab.

If you don't want to take a taxi, you can go by bus or you can take the subway. The subway is quick, and it's cheap, but parts of it are old and dirty. Lights don't always work, and there are often fires on the track. On some subway lines, there are new, clean, silver trains. But you can't see the color of the old trains easily. There is too much dirt and too much graffiti, inside and outside.

People are afraid of the New York subway. On any day of the week, there are nearly 40 crimes. There are also many people in the subway who are drunk or sick or very poor. For a long time, the subway has been a sad and dangerous place. But now it's changing. New York is working hard to make its subway cleaner and safer. The New Yorkers are pleased about that. They need their subway. It runs 24 hours a day and carries a billion people a year. New York wouldn't be the same without it.

Left: A busy New York street.
Top right: Graffiti on old subway trains.
Bottom right: New subway trains.

FROM COAST TO COAST

Before the days of the automobile, trains were the best way to travel. Roads were bad, and horses were slow. There were few rivers and riverboats. Trains were new, safe, and fast.

The story of the railroads is one of the great stories of American history. In 1866, two big railroad companies agreed to build a railroad all the way across America. The Union Pacific started from the east, and the Central Pacific started from the west. Ten thousand men worked on both sides. They built the railroad over rivers and valleys, across the prairie and across the Rocky Mountains. After three years, the two sides met, and the first trains began to run from coast to coast.

The railroad caused the building of many small towns in the Midwest. They grew up at railroad stopping places. The railroad was the most interesting thing in town. At that time, of course, there were no movies or television. In their free time, people just watched the trains go past.

When the highways came, the railroads were less important. In many places, trains stopped running. It was even worse when air travel began. You could fly from New York to San Francisco in a few hours. It took more than two days by train.

Now, people are choosing to travel by train again. Gas is expensive, and driving is tiring. When you go by air, you have to drive out of town to an airport and wait a long time for your plane. But trains go from one city center to another.

American trains can be very modern and comfortable. Some of them have restaurants and bars. Some have bedrooms for families to sleep in. Trains that go through beautiful parts of the country sometimes have glass roofs. You can look all around and enjoy the wonderful forests and mountains.

But there are problems too. Many trains are old. They break down or arrive late. Stations are not always clean and friendly places. It's the same all over the world. If you pay to go on the best trains, you get the best. If you travel cheaply, you must expect the worst.

Left: The Union Pacific railroad meets the Central Pacific railroad in Utah on 10 May 1869.

Top right: A modern American train—the "Empire Builder."

Bottom right: A train with a glass roof.

THE LONGEST TRAIL OF ALL

Do you like walking? I don't mean short walks to the store and home again. I mean real walking. If you do like it, you will enjoy hiking along the Appalachian Trail. How long does it take? Well, fast hikers can do it in six months. Some people take a lot longer. One sixty-year-old man took seventeen years to walk along the whole trail from north to south.

The Appalachian Trail is long—2,096 miles long. It starts in Georgia, in the South, and finishes in Maine, on the Canadian border. It's one of the longest hiking trails in the world. It's also one of the most beautiful and interesting.

Only about a hundred people hike the whole trail every year. But thousands walk along a short part of it. The most beautiful parts, perhaps, are in Tennessee and Virginia. In the summer, there are crowds of people walking, talking, and making friends. Along the path, they can enjoy the birdsong and the wild flowers. Some lucky hikers might even see a bear.

Most people hike about nine or ten miles a day. They go from one "shelter" to another. They can sleep

at the shelter and cook their food. The shelters are free.

Americans like to travel by car at home and in the city. But many of them love to hike and go horseback riding during their vacations. The Appalachian Trail is not the only place for hikers. The U.S.'s wonderful national parks are full of them in the summertime. Some people like to stay at one campground, go out from it in the morning, and come back in the evening. Other people pack food and clothes for a few days and carry them on their backs. This is called "backpacking." Backpackers can go where they like and stay in a different cabin or campground every night.

Some people, of course, prefer horseback riding to hiking. In many of the parks, like the Rocky Mountains National Park, or Yellowstone, in Wyoming, you can rent horses. Then you can sit quietly and enjoy the beautiful views. Your horse will do the walking for you.

Left: Young hikers with their backpacks on the trail.
Above: Horseback riding in Tucson, Arizona.

IT'S CHEAPER BY BUS

You don't find millionaires on buses. Or movie stars. Or rich lawyers. Or Wall Street bankers. But you'll find Mr. and Ms. America. Good people, bad people, happy people, sad people, and people with stories to tell. They all go by bus. It's cheap. It's the cheapest ride in the U.S.

The buses go, night and day, right across America. On the longest trips, you have to change the time on your watch. Don't forget, the United States is *big*. When it's midnight in New York, it's only 9 o'clock in San Francisco. When it's 2 o'clock in Denver, it's 3 o'clock in Kansas City. This means you have to read the bus times very, very carefully.

Bus stations are not always the nicest places. They are full of tired people, crying children, busy ticket sellers, and empty Coca-Cola cans. But climb on the bus, and it's good. The seats go back like the ones on airplanes. The windows are made of dark glass to keep you cool. There's a toilet. There are people who want to talk to you. And outside, there's America. Mile after mile of it. Dry red and yellow deserts. Flat green wheat fields. High snowy mountains. Great busy cities. Small towns and big farmhouses. Sandy beaches and ocean waves.

Some buses go 1,000 miles in one day. And at the end of the day, you can stay on the bus if you like, and sleep on it all through the night. You can sleep all day too. But don't go to sleep when you're crossing the Rockies. The mountains, rivers, and valleys are too beautiful. And you probably won't go to sleep when you're crossing Death Valley, in California. In the summer, it's very, very hot. It can be dangerous too. You can't live long in Death Valley without water. If cars or buses break down there, there's a big problem.

If you don't want to sleep on the bus, you can always find a motel. The most interesting ones are the small family ones. The world of the great highways is their life. The motel owners give beds to tired travelers and worried people looking for work. They cook steaks for truckers, and hamburgers for tourists. They smile at lovers and watch carefully the man with the gun. Their doors are always open when the bus comes into town.

Top left: A Greyhound poster from the 1930s.
Bottom left: A Greyhound bus on the road.
Above: A bus station in Texas.

THE FLYING BUSINESS

Sixty years ago, you needed days to travel from the East Coast to the West Coast. But now, you can do it in a few hours.

Travel by air is much cheaper now than it was. There are many airlines who want new customers. They keep prices low. In some airports, there are up to thirty different airline companies. Travelers can choose among TWA, Pan Am, Eastern Airlines, Braniff, Continental, Delta, American Airlines, and many, many more.

Americans often live a long way from their families. There are young women from Chicago who are studying in Boston. There are old men in Sun City, Arizona, who were born in Minneapolis. These people often leave their families when they move to a new place. But sometimes, families want to be together again. Thanksgiving, in November, and Christmas, in December, are two very important family holidays. Then, millions of people are in a hurry to fly home.

Airports are crowded, and planes are full. It's a problem for the people who work for the airlines.

The problems are growing all the time. Americans take hundreds of millions of flights every year. More and more planes want to land and take off at the airports. There are often "traffic jams" in the sky. Accidents can easily happen. Planes are often late, and passengers get angry.

What can the airlines do to make flying easier? They can build bigger airports, of course. But the airports will soon fill up with more planes. They can make flying more expensive. But then one airline will cut prices again, and all of them will have to do the same. There really isn't an answer to the problem. Americans have always loved to travel, and they always will. The roads will go on taking more and more and more cars, and more and more people will travel by air.

But what will happen when there is no more oil and gas?

Top left: Tired travelers picking up their baggage.
Left: Airplanes on the ground.

AIR, WIND, AND SNOW

Cars, buses, airplanes, and trains are good enough for some of us. But there are people who always want something new. There are a lot of those people in the U.S. The country is so big, with so much land, that it's easy to try new ideas.

Some people like flying in a hot-air balloon. It's a wonderful way to see the country. It's cool, it's quiet, and you can feel the wind on your face. It's even better if you do it with other people. Every year, there's a balloon festival in Albuquerque,

New Mexico. At sunrise, hundreds of beautiful colored balloons fly up into the air together. If you see it, you will never forget it.

If you want to stay nearer to Earth, you can try windskating. It's not quite the same as flying. But when you jump in a strong wind, you can go a long way off the ground. Windskating is very popular in California. There are parking lots near the sea that are ten miles long. They are perfect for windskating. All you need is a pair of roller skates and your sail. The wind will carry you along. Some windskaters go at 50 miles per hour. That's fast!

Windskating is great in sunny California, but in Alaska there's a different kind of fun. Up there, in the cold, cold north, the snow is sometimes 15 feet deep. You can't use cars and buses there. The Inuit people of Alaska used to travel on dog sleds. They still do, but now, other Americans have joined them. Every year, in February, there are the World Championship Dog Sled Races in Anchorage, Alaska.

Dog sleds are not the only things that can travel across the snow. For lazy people, there are snowmobiles. They are light and comfortable. On your snowmobile, you can travel miles in one day, and, if you're lucky, you can see foxes, bears, and other wild animals.

For people who are not so lazy, there are skis. Of course, it's hard work skiing over all that snow. But it certainly keeps you warm.

Top left: Balloons at Albuquerque, New Mexico.
Left: Windskaters in Oregon.
Above: Dogsledding in Alaska.

ON THE BIG-SEA-WATERS

Native Americans have always built canoes and traveled along the thousands of miles of the Great Lakes and rivers of North America. Their canoes are light and fast. They are easy to carry over land and useful for fishing on the water.

Henry Longfellow, a nineteenth-century poet, wrote a long poem about Hiawatha, a great Native American hero who built a canoe. In it, he traveled away to the west across Lake Superior ("Gitchee Gumee") to fight the terrible Megissogwon. An old woman, Nokomis, showed him where to go:

"On the shores of Gitchee Gumee
Of the shining Big-Sea-Water
Stood Nokomis, the old woman,
Pointing with her finger
 westward,
O'er (over) the water pointing
 westward
To the purple clouds of sunset."

You can still see canoes on the Great Lakes, but the people in them are tourists from the cities. Few people use boats for real travel anymore. It's faster and easier to go by plane or by car. But many people still like going down a river when they're on vacation.

For young people who like adventure, there are the fast and dangerous waters of mountain rivers. The Salmon River in Idaho is a favorite place for white water rafting. The Native Americans called this river "the River of No Return." They could go down it, but they could not get up it again.

All kinds of boats go up and down the sleepy, slow rivers of Louisiana, in the warm South. You can hire one if you want to visit these hot, muddy rivers, called "bayous." You'll see many kinds of birds, fish, and even alligators.

The Mississippi, together with its mother, the Missouri, is the longest river in the world. It was once the most important "road" in the U.S. There are still a few of the old boats on the Mississippi, but you can ride on them for only a short time. On these lovely boats, it's easy to remember the old days, when life was slower and there was always plenty of time.

Top left: Fun and danger on a white water raft.
Bottom left: Hiawatha, Longfellow's Native American hero, in his canoe.
Above: Fishing on the bayous of Louisiana.

TRAVEL IS GOOD FOR YOU

Americans think that travel is good for you. Some even think it can help one of the country's worst problems—crime.

Crime worries a lot of people. Every year, the number of crimes goes up and up. And many criminals are young. Most of them—85 percent—are boys. They often come from sad homes, with only one parent or no parents at all. There are problems with alcohol and drugs.

There are many young criminals in prison. But prison doesn't change them. Sixty to seventy percent will go back to crime when they come out of prison.

One man, Bob Burton, thought of a new idea. In the old days, young men had to live a difficult life on the road. They learned to be strong and brave, and to help their friends in times of danger. This helped them to grow into men. So Bob Burton started "Vision Quest." He takes young criminals on a long, long journey with horses and wagons, 3,000 miles through seven states. They are on the road for more than a year.

The young people on Vision Quest (boys and a few girls) all have bad problems. Most of them have already spent time in prison. This is their last chance.

It's hard work on the road. The day starts before the sun comes up.

The boys and girls have to feed the horses. Some of them have never loved anyone before. But they can love their horse. That love can help them to a new life.

"I like my animal," wrote one young criminal. "He's my best friend. When I want to play, I go play with him. Playing is when he's standing up, and I try to push him back and he tries to bite me. I like my animal. The way I see it, that's my family."

When the animals are ready, the camp moves on. They travel twenty miles a day. Sometimes people shout at each other, and break the rules. Then the leaders have to spend a lot of time talking, listening, and making things right again.

Not all the young people on Vision Quest will leave crime behind them. Thirty or forty percent will one day be in prison again. But that's a lot better than sixty or seventy percent. Bob Burton is right. Travel can be good for you.

Even today, Americans still say, "Go west, young man."

Left: Making a camp on the trail.
Above: The long trail away from prison.

Addison Wesley Longman Limited,
Edinburgh Gate, Harlow,
Essex CM20 2JE, England
and Associated Companies throughout the world.

© Longman Group UK Limited 1989
All rights reserved; no part of this publication
may be reproduced, stored in a retrieval system,
or transmitted in any form or by any means,
electronic, mechanical, photocopying, recording
or otherwise, without the prior written permission
of the Publishers.

First published 1989
Third impression 1996

Set in Linotron 202 Times Roman 11/13pt

Printed in China
SWTC/03

ISBN 0 582 01715 7

Acknowledgement

We are grateful to the following for permission to reproduce copyright photographs:

All-Sport (UK) Limited for page 27; Amtrak for page 19 (top and bottom); Art Directors Photo Library for pages 6 (top) and 24/25; Colorific Photo Library Limited for pages 11 and 14; The Library of Congress for page 3 (bottom); Sally and Richard Greenhill for pages 5, 6 (bottom), 9 and 16; The Hulton Picture company/Bettman for page 3 (top); The Image Bank for page 17 (top); Impact Photos for page 31; The Metropolitan Transports Authority for page 17 (bottom); Peter Newarks Western Americana Photo Library for pages 2, 18 and 28 (bottom); Peterbilt Motors Company for page 15 (bottom); The Photographers Library for page 7; Pictor International Limited for pages 4 and 20; Frank Spooner Pictures for pages 15 (top) and 26 (bottom; Tony Stone Photo Library/London for page 10 and Tony Stone/ Click Chicago for pages 8 (left), 22 (bottom), 24, 26 (top) and 29; Topham Picture Library for page 22 (top) and Topham Picture Library/The Image Works, Inc., for page 23; Visionquest for page 30; Darryl Williams for pages 8 (right) and 12/13; Zefa Picture Library (UK) Limited for page 21 and Zefa/The Stock Market for page 28 (top).

Cover photograph by Zefa Picture Library (UK) Limited.

Picture Research by Sandie Huskinson-Rolfe